Romeo a

WILLIAM SHAKESPEARE

Level 3

Retold by Anne Collins
Series Editors: Andy Hopkins and Jocelyn Potter

Pearson Education Limited
Edinburgh Gate, Harlow,
Essex CM20 2JE, England
and Associated Companies throughout the world.

ISBN: 978-1-4058-5546-4

First published by Penguin Books 2002
This edition published 2008

12

Text copyright © Penguin Books Ltd 2002
This edition copyright © Pearson Education Ltd 2008
Illustrations copyright © Giovanni Caselli at agile@authors.co.uk

Typeset by Graphicraft Ltd, Hong Kong
Set in 11/14pt Bembo
Printed in China
SWTC/12

*All rights reserved; no part of this publication may be reproduced, stored
in a retrieval system, or transmitted in any form or by any means,
electronic, mechanical, photocopying, recording or otherwise, without the
prior written permission of the Publishers.*

Published by Pearson Education Ltd

Every effort has been made to trace the copyright holders and we apologise in advance for any unintentional omissions. We would be pleased to insert the appropriate acknowledgement in any subsequent edition of this publication.

For a complete list of the titles available in the Pearson English Readers series, please visit www.pearsonenglishreaders.com. Alternatively, write to your local Pearson Education office or to Pearson English Readers Marketing Department, Pearson Education, Edinburgh Gate, Harlow, Essex CM20 2JE, England.

Contents

	page
Introduction	v
The Characters in the Play	viii
Act 1 The Capulets and the Montagues	1
Act 2 Marriage Plans	11
Act 3 Murder and Banishment	22
Act 4 The Sweetest Flower	37
Act 5 Death in the Vault	44
Activities	54

Introduction

'The sun, from sadness, will not shine at all today. There was never a sadder story than this story of Romeo and Juliet.'

Romeo and Juliet is one of the most famous love stories in the world. Today, more than four hundred years after it was written, it is as popular as in Shakespeare's time. Perhaps this is because the play is more than a great love story. It is also about murder, life and death, happiness and sadness, problems between parents and children, and the terrible hate between two great families. There are six deaths in *Romeo and Juliet*! Some parts of the play are quiet and romantic, some are exciting, some are funny and some are very sad.

Many of Shakespeare's plays take place in countries outside England like Italy, Greece or Denmark. The characters in *Romeo and Juliet* live in the famous city of Verona in the north of Italy.

The story is about two important families of the town, the Capulets and the Montagues. These families are great enemies. We are not told the reason for their hate – only that it is not new. They are always fighting in the streets of Verona, and this is a great problem for the Prince and the people of the town. Then Romeo, the only son of the Montagues, falls in love with Juliet, the only daughter of the Capulets. Their love ends their families' hate – but only with their deaths.

Shakespeare has given us some beautiful language in *Romeo and Juliet*, and also some wonderful characters. Friar Laurence, wise and kind, tries to help the lovers. Mercutio, Romeo's friend, laughs and jokes about love. Lord Capulet, Juliet's father, doesn't understand his daughter. The Nurse never stops talking. Angry Tybalt is always ready for a fight, and Benvolio, Romeo's cousin, only wants peace.

William Shakespeare is the most famous writer of plays in the English language. He was born in Stratford-upon-Avon on 26 April 1564, in the time of Queen Elizabeth I, and died on 23 April 1616. He wrote thirty-seven plays and many famous poems. His plays are about different subjects. Some of them are about famous people in history. Others are stories from the literature of the time. He was not only a writer of plays – he also acted in them. His plays were very popular and successful.

In 1582 Shakespeare married Anne Hathaway, and they had three children – a boy and two girls. By 1597 he was rich enough to buy New Place, the largest house in Stratford.

Shakespeare began writing *Romeo and Juliet* in 1594, when he was about thirty years old. The idea for the story was not Shakespeare's. It came from a story in 1562 by Arthur Brooke about two young lovers who killed themselves. Shakespeare took Brooke's story and wrote his play around it, but he added new characters too.

In Shakespeare's time, the actors were all men. So the part of Juliet was played by a boy. This is quite hard for us to imagine now! Many great actors and actresses have wanted to play Romeo or Juliet in the theatre. There have also been films and television plays. In 1968 Franco Zeffirelli made a beautiful film in Italy with two unknown young actors, Leonard Whiting and Olivia Hussey. Sometimes *Romeo and Juliet* is shown as a modern story taking place in today's world. In 1996 the actor Leonardo DiCaprio played Romeo in a very different kind of *Romeo and Juliet* from Shakespeare's. In this film, the story and characters were moved from the old Italian city of Verona to a very modern city called Verona Beach.

Reading and acting the play

You can read *Romeo and Juliet* silently, like every other story in a book. You will have to imagine the places, the characters' clothes and their voices from the words on the page.

But Shakespeare did not write *Romeo and Juliet* as literature for reading. He wrote it for actors on a theatre stage. You can read the play in a group with other people. This is very different from silent reading. You can speak the words and bring the characters to life. They can sound happy, sad or angry. You can add silences and important noises, like the sound of knocking. You can also stop and discuss the play. What does this character mean? Why does he/she say that?

But you can have more fun if you act the play. *Romeo and Juliet* has a lot of movement and colour. There are wonderful love scenes, but there are exciting fights too. There is music and dancing. There are scenes with a crowd, and scenes with just two people. The characters can show their feelings by their words, but also by their actions. Romeo can show his love for Juliet, Tybalt can show his hate for Romeo, and Lord Capulet can show his changing feelings towards his daughter.

If you act *Romeo and Juliet*, the scenes should look different – the town square in Verona, Juliet's bedroom, Friar Laurence's garden and the Capulets' vault. You should also think about stage equipment – swords, a rope, a bottle of poison, a letter. *Romeo and Juliet* has a lot of characters. Some have large parts, like Romeo, Juliet and Friar Laurence – others, like the Doctor in Mantua, only have a few short lines. Some characters don't speak, but their actions on stage are important. How many townspeople do you need? How many guests will there be at Lord Capulet's party?

Romeo and Juliet is a wonderful play. You can read it or you can act it. But have fun and enjoy it!

The Characters in the Play

PRINCE ESCALUS, Prince of Verona
MERCUTIO, a relative of the Prince and a friend of Romeo
PARIS, a relative of the Prince; he wants to marry Juliet
SERVANT, Paris's servant

LORD MONTAGUE, head of the Montague family
LADY MONTAGUE, Lord Montague's wife
ROMEO, Lord Montague's son
BENVOLIO, Romeo's cousin; Romeo and Mercutio's friend
ABRAM, a servant of the Montague family
BALTHASAR, Romeo's servant

LORD CAPULET, head of the Capulet family
LADY CAPULET, Lord Capulet's wife
JULIET, Lord Capulet's daughter
TYBALT, Juliet's cousin
NURSE, Juliet's nurse
COUSIN CAPULET, Lord Capulet's old cousin
PETER, Lord Capulet's servant
SAMPSON and GREGORY, servants of the Capulet family

FRIAR LAURENCE, a religious friar
FRIAR JOHN, assistant to Friar Laurence
DOCTOR, from the town of Mantua
SIX GUARDS, guarding Verona at night
TOWNSPEOPLE of Verona
SERVANTS, the Prince of Verona's servants
YOUNG MEN IN MASKS, friends of Romeo and Mercutio
TYBALT'S FRIENDS
GUESTS at Lord Capulet's party

Act 1   The Capulets and the Montagues

Scene 1   The town square in Verona

[*Sampson and Gregory arrive, carrying swords.*]

SAMPSON: If I meet any of those Montague dogs today, I'm ready to attack them.
GREGORY: Well, get your sword out then. Here come two of Montague's servants.

[*Abram and Balthasar arrive.*]

SAMPSON: I'll make a rude face at them and make them angry.
ABRAM: Are you making a rude face at us, sir?
SAMPSON [*to Gregory*]: Is the law on our side if I say 'yes'?
GREGORY: No, it isn't.
SAMPSON [*to Abram*]: No, I'm not making a rude face at you, sir. But ... I *am* making a rude face.
GREGORY: Are you trying to start a fight with us, sir?
ABRAM: Start a fight, sir? No, sir.
SAMPSON: Well, if you *do* want to start a fight, I'm ready for you. My master is a good man – as good as yours.

[*Benvolio arrives from one side, and Tybalt from the other.*]

ABRAM: Not a *better* man?
GREGORY [*to Sampson*]: Say 'better'. Here comes one of our master's relatives.
SAMPSON [*to Abram*]: He's a better man, sir.
ABRAM: You're lying!
SAMPSON: Take out your swords! Let's fight them, Gregory!

[*Sampson and Gregory get out their swords and start fighting.*]

BENVOLIO: Stop fighting, you stupid men! Put your swords away. You don't know what you're doing.

TYBALT [*getting out his sword*]: So you're in this fight too, Benvolio? Turn, and prepare to die!

BENVOLIO: I'm only trying to keep the peace. Put your sword away. Or use it to stop these men fighting.

TYBALT: Your sword is out, but you talk about peace? I hate that word, as I hate all Montagues. [*attacking him*] Take this!

[*Tybalt and Benvolio fight. Three or four townspeople of Verona walk past and start fighting too.*]

TOWNSPEOPLE: Down with the Capulets! Down with the Montagues!

[*Lord Capulet and his wife arrive.*]

LORD CAPULET: What's all this noise? [*to Sampson*] Go and bring me my long sword!

LADY CAPULET: Why are you calling for a sword?

[*Lord Montague and his wife arrive.*]

LORD CAPULET: Bring me my sword, I say! Here's old Montague. He has *his* sword out, ready to fight.

LORD MONTAGUE [*to his wife*]: Don't hold me back!

LADY MONTAGUE [*holding him*]: You're not going to fight.

[*Prince Escalus arrives with his servants.*]

PRINCE: Enemies of peace, throw your swords to the ground! This is the third time, Capulet and Montague, that fighting between your families has broken the peace of our streets. Go home, everybody. Come with me now, Capulet. Come and see me later, Montague.

[*All leave except Lord and Lady Montague and Benvolio.*]

LORD MONTAGUE: Who started this fight? Speak, Benvolio. Were you here when it began?

BENVOLIO: Your servants and Capulet's servants were fighting. I tried to stop them, but then angry Tybalt started fighting too. More and more people came and joined us. Then the Prince came and stopped everything.

LADY MONTAGUE: Have you seen Romeo today? I'm very glad he wasn't at this terrible fight.

BENVOLIO: Madam, an hour before the sun came up, I went for a walk. I saw Romeo walking near the west side of the city. But he ran away and hid in a wood.

LORD MONTAGUE: People have often seen him there early in the morning, looking very sad. But when the sun comes up, my son goes home. He shuts himself in his room.

BENVOLIO: My noble uncle, do you know the reason?

LORD MONTAGUE: I and many other friends have asked him, but he keeps it a secret. We can't help him until we learn the reason for his sadness.

[*Romeo arrives.*]

BENVOLIO: Here he comes. I'll find out what his problem is.

LORD MONTAGUE: I hope he tells you the true reason. [*to his wife*] Let's go, Madam.

[*Lord and Lady Montague leave.*]

BENVOLIO: Good morning, cousin.

ROMEO: Is it still so early?

BENVOLIO: It's only about nine o'clock.

ROMEO: Ah, sad hours pass slowly. Was that my father who hurried away from here?

BENVOLIO: Yes. What sadness makes your hours long, Romeo? Are you in love?

ROMEO: Yes, but I love a lady who doesn't love me. [*looking around*] But what terrible fight has happened here? No, don't tell me – I've heard it all before. Hate is the reason for this fight, but I'm suffering more from love.

BENVOLIO: I'm very sorry that you're so unhappy. Tell me, who are you in love with?

ROMEO: I love a beautiful woman called Rosaline. But she isn't interested in me.

BENVOLIO: Listen to me – forget about her.

ROMEO: Oh, tell me how I *can* forget about her!

BENVOLIO: Use your eyes. Look at other beautiful women.

ROMEO: If I compare other beautiful women with her, I only think about her more.

BENVOLIO: I can teach you how to forget her.

[*Romeo and Benvolio leave.*]

Scene 2   A street near the Capulets' house

[*Lord Capulet and Paris arrive with Peter, Capulet's servant.*]

LORD CAPULET: But Montague has had to promise to keep the peace too. That isn't difficult for old men like us.

PARIS: You are both men from noble families. It's a pity you have been enemies for so long. But now, sir, what do you say to my hopes of marrying your daughter, Juliet?

LORD CAPULET: The same thing as I have said before. My daughter is very young – not yet fourteen. She won't be ready for marriage for two more years.

PARIS: There are happy mothers who are younger than she is.

LORD CAPULET: Yes, but that isn't a good thing. All my other children have died; Juliet is my only hope. But win her heart, Paris. If she agrees to marry you, I'll agree to it too. Tonight I'm having a party for my dearest friends. You're very welcome to join us. You'll see ladies as beautiful as stars lighting up the dark sky. See them all, listen to them all. Then you can decide if you still prefer Juliet. [*giving a paper to Peter*] Go and find the people on this list. Invite them to my party this evening.

[*Lord Capulet and Paris leave.*]

PETER: Find the people on this list! How can I do that? I can't read their names. I'll have to ask somebody.

[*Romeo and Benvolio arrive.*]

BENVOLIO: I tell you, find a new love and forget your old one. A new pain or sadness will drive the old pain away.

ROMEO: The pain of my love is more serious than that. [*to Peter*] Good evening.

PETER: Good evening. [*showing him the paper*] Can you read, sir?

ROMEO: Yes, I can read. [*reading the paper*] 'Signor* Martino and his wife and daughters. Signor Anselm and his beautiful sisters. Signor Placentio and his lovely daughters. Mercutio and his brother Valentine. My uncle Capulet, his wife and daughters. The beautiful Rosaline. Signor Valentio and his cousin Tybalt.' A nice group of people. Where are they invited to?

PETER: To my master's house. My master is the great rich Capulet. If you aren't one of the Montague family, come too. Have a drink with us. Goodbye! [*He leaves.*]

BENVOLIO: Your great love, Rosaline, is going to be at this party. Go there, and compare her to the other beautiful women of Verona. Then you'll see that she's ugly.

ROMEO: Another woman more beautiful than my love? There has never been anyone more beautiful in the world. I'll go to the party, but only to see Rosaline.

[*Romeo and Benvolio leave.*]

---

*Signor: the Italian word for Mr

Scene 3   Juliet's bedroom in the Capulets' house

[*Lady Capulet and Juliet's Nurse come in.*]

LADY CAPULET: Nurse, where's my daughter? Call her to me.
NURSE: I've already told her to come. Where *is* that girl? Juliet!

[*Juliet comes in.*]

JULIET: What is it? Who's calling me?
NURSE: Your mother.
JULIET: Here I am, mother. What do you want?
LADY CAPULET: Nurse, leave us alone – we have to talk privately. [*The Nurse looks sad and starts to go out.*] Nurse, come back – you can hear our discussion. [*The Nurse returns, looking happy.*] You know how old Juliet is.
NURSE: Yes, of course! She'll be fourteen in July. My daughter Susan and she were about the same age. Well, Susan's in heaven – she was too good for me. But as I said, in July Juliet will be fourteen. [*to Juliet*] You were the prettiest baby that I ever nursed. If I can see you married, I'll be happy.
LADY CAPULET: Marriage is exactly the subject that I want to talk about. [*to Juliet*] Tell me, daughter Juliet, how do you feel about getting married?
JULIET [*surprised*]: I've never thought about marriage.
LADY CAPULET: Well, think about it now. Younger ladies than you from noble families in Verona are already mothers. I became your mother at about the same age as you are now. Listen – the fine gentleman Paris would like to marry you.
NURSE: He's a perfect picture of a man, young lady!
LADY CAPULET: Verona's summer has no finer flower.
NURSE: Yes, he's like a flower, a beautiful flower.
LADY CAPULET [*to Juliet*]: But what do you say? Can you love this gentleman? You'll see him tonight at our party. Look

closely at his handsome face. You can read his feelings by looking in his eyes. Can you welcome his love?

JULIET: I'll look at him, and try to like him.

[*Peter suddenly runs in.*]

PETER [*excitedly*]: Madam, the guests have arrived and dinner is ready. You are called for, and my young lady is asked for, and Nurse is needed in the kitchen.

LADY CAPULET: We're coming. [*Peter goes out.*] Juliet, Paris is waiting for you.

NURSE: Go, girl. Look for happy days – and nights.

[*Juliet and the Nurse go out.*]

Scene 4 A street near the Capulets' house

[*Romeo, Mercutio and Benvolio arrive with two or three other young men. They are carrying masks and lights.*]

ROMEO: Shall we introduce ourselves at the party by making a speech? Or shall we just go in without saying anything?

BENVOLIO: Let's not make a speech. They can judge us as they want. We'll have a dance and then leave.

ROMEO: Give me a light. I don't want to dance. My heart is too sad and heavy. I prefer to carry a light.

MERCUTIO: No, my dear Romeo, you must dance.

ROMEO: Not I, believe me. You have light dancing shoes. But my feet feel tied to the ground. I can't move.

MERCUTIO: But you're a lover! Love can carry you high above ordinary things.

ROMEO [*sadly*]: No, you're wrong. Love is a heavy weight that's pressing down on me.

MERCUTIO: Then get on top of love! [*taking a mask*] Give me a mask! I have an ugly face but this mask will hide it.

BENVOLIO: Come, let's knock and go in. When we get inside, start dancing, everybody!

ROMEO: Give me a light. People with light hearts can dance. I'll just carry a light and watch.

MERCUTIO: Come on, our lights are burning out.

ROMEO: We're only trying to have some fun at this party. But it's unwise to go there.

MERCUTIO: Why? What do you mean?

ROMEO: I had a bad dream tonight.

MERCUTIO: Me too.

ROMEO: What was your dream about?

MERCUTIO: That dreams are often not true.

BENVOLIO: Come, they've finished dinner. We'll arrive too late.

ROMEO: Too early, I'm afraid. I have a feeling that this party tonight is going to be the start of something terrible. Perhaps it will even result in my death. But let's go!

[*All the young men put on their masks and leave.*]

Scene 5 A large room in the Capulets' house

[*Lord and Lady Capulet, Juliet, the Nurse and all the guests are there. Romeo and his friends arrive, wearing masks.*]

LORD CAPULET [*to his guests*]: Welcome, everybody! [*to Romeo and his friends*] Welcome, gentlemen! These lovely ladies will have a dance with you. There was a time when I too wore a mask. [*laughing*] I can remember speaking soft words into a beautiful lady's ear. You are very welcome, gentlemen! Let's have some music. [*Music plays, and the guests start to dance.*] More light! [*to his cousin*] Sit down, cousin Capulet. Our dancing days have ended. How long is it since you and I wore a mask?

COUSIN CAPULET: Thirty years.

LORD CAPULET: What? It can't be so long. It was at Lucentio's wedding, about twenty-five years ago.

COUSIN CAPULET: It's more, it's more. His son is older than that. His son is thirty.

LORD CAPULET [*surprised*]: Are you sure?

[*Romeo suddenly notices Juliet dancing.*]

ROMEO [*to himself*]: Who is that beautiful lady, shining so brightly in the dark night? She is too beautiful for ordinary life, too special for this world! She is like a lovely white bird in a group of ugly black ones. At the end of this dance, I'll see where she stands. I'll try and touch her lovely hand with my rough one. Was I in love before? No – not until tonight.

TYBALT [*standing near Romeo and listening*]: This man has the voice of a Montague. Has he come here in that stupid mask to make fun of our party? I'll get my sword.

LORD CAPULET [*coming towards Tybalt*]: What's the matter, Tybalt? Why are you looking so angry?

TYBALT [*pointing to Romeo*]: Uncle, that man is a Montague, one of our enemies. He's come here to make fun of us.

LORD CAPULET: It's young Romeo, isn't it?

TYBALT: Yes.

LORD CAPULET: Be calm, dear cousin, leave him alone. He's acting like a gentleman. People in Verona say he's a nice young man. I don't want to hurt him here in my house. So be pleasant and put away those angry looks.

TYBALT: I hate him.

LORD CAPULET: Be polite to him! Am I the master here, or are you? Do you want to make trouble for my guests?

TYBALT: It's not right, uncle . . .

LORD CAPULET: That's enough! You're a rude and silly boy. I know what I'm doing. [*to servants*] Bring more lights! [*to Tybalt*] Now go! Be quiet or I'll make you quiet.

TYBALT: I'll go. But something bad will happen as a result of these unwelcome guests at our party. [*He goes out.*]

ROMEO [*to Juliet, touching her hand and looking into her eyes*]: If I touch your beautiful hand with mine, please forgive me. My touch is rough, but I can make it smooth with a kiss.

JULIET [*giving Romeo her hand and looking into his eyes*]: But, sir, the touch of your hand isn't rough at all. Let's join our hands together. Like this. [*She puts her hand against Romeo's hand.*]

ROMEO: Please can I kiss you?

JULIET: Yes.

ROMEO: Don't move. [*He kisses her.*]

JULIET: You are very good at kissing.

NURSE [*hurrying towards Juliet*]: Madam, your mother wants to talk to you.

[*Juliet leaves Romeo and goes to her mother.*]

ROMEO: Who is her mother?

NURSE: Her mother is the lady of the house, of course. And a very good, wise and kind lady. I nursed her daughter – the girl you talked to just now. I tell you ... her husband will be a lucky man! [*She goes away.*]

ROMEO: Is she a Capulet? That's terrible news!

BENVOLIO [*coming towards Romeo*]: Let's go.

LORD CAPULET: Good night, gentlemen. Thank you all for coming. [*to servants*] Bring more lights! Let's go to bed. It's getting late.

[*Everybody except Juliet and the Nurse goes out.*]

JULIET: Come here, Nurse. Who's that gentleman over there?

NURSE: That's old Tiberio's son.

JULIET: Who's the man going out of the door now?

NURSE: I think that's young Petruchio.

JULIET: Who's that man who didn't want to dance?

NURSE: I don't know.

JULIET: Go and ask his name. [*to herself*] If he's married, I'll never have a wedding-bed, only a grave.

[*The Nurse goes to ask Romeo's name, then comes back.*]

NURSE: His name is Romeo and he's a Montague – the only son of your family's great enemy.
JULIET: My only love is the son of my only enemy! I didn't know that when I met him. But now it's too late!
NURSE: What's this, what's this?
JULIET: Nothing – just a silly joke that somebody told me tonight.
NURSE: Let's go. The guests have all gone home.

[*Juliet and the Nurse go out.*]

Act 2   Marriage Plans

Scene 1   The Capulets' garden, with Juliet's bedroom above

[*Romeo comes in, alone.*]

ROMEO: How can I leave when the centre of my world is here?

[*Benvolio and Mercutio come in. Romeo runs away and hides.*]

BENVOLIO: Romeo! My cousin Romeo! Romeo!
MERCUTIO: He's clever. I'm sure he's gone home to bed.
BENVOLIO: He ran this way and jumped over the garden wall. Call him, dear Mercutio.
MERCUTIO: I'll use Rosaline's name, and talk about her bright eyes, her beautiful feet, her lovely straight legs ...
BENVOLIO: If he hears you, he'll be angry with you.
MERCUTIO: No, that won't make him angry. I'm only using her name to find him.
BENVOLIO: He's hidden himself in the darkness of those trees.
MERCUTIO [*calling*]: Romeo, good night! [*to Benvolio*] This ground is too cold to sleep on. Come, shall we go home?

BENVOLIO: Yes, let's go. He doesn't want us to find him.

[*Benvolio and Mercutio leave.*]

ROMEO [*coming back*]: Mercutio laughs at things that he doesn't understand. He has never felt those things. [*Juliet opens the window of her room, above. He looks up.*] But wait! What's that light, shining from that window? It's the east, and Juliet is the sun! She's much more beautiful than the pale moon. It's my lady! Oh, it's my love! But she doesn't know that she's my love. [*Juliet says something to herself.*] She's speaking, but she isn't saying anything. I'll answer her. But no, I'm wrong to do that. She isn't speaking to me. Her eyes shine like two of the most beautiful stars in heaven. But the light in her face shines even more brightly than her eyes.

JULIET: Oh!

ROMEO [*to himself*]: She speaks. Oh, speak again, beautiful lady!

JULIET: Oh Romeo, Romeo – why are you called Romeo? Say that you aren't your father's son. Say that Montague isn't your name. Or if you don't want to do that, promise to be my love. And I won't be a Capulet any longer.

ROMEO [*to himself*]: Shall I listen to more, or shall I speak?

JULIET: It's only your name that is my enemy. You're yourself, not a Montague. What *is* a 'Montague'? It isn't a hand, or a foot, or an arm, or a face. If we call a rose by a different name, it will still smell just as sweet. So Romeo will still be perfect without the name 'Romeo'. Romeo, throw away that name. And in its place, take all of me.

ROMEO: Only say that I'm your love. I'll never be Romeo again.

JULIET [*frightened*]: Who are you?

ROMEO [*showing himself*]: I don't know how to tell you my name. I hate my name because it's your enemy.

JULIET: I've only listened to a few words, but I know your voice. Aren't you Romeo, and a Montague?

ROMEO: I'm neither of those things, beautiful lady, if you don't like them.

JULIET: How did you get in here? Why did you come? The garden walls are high and difficult to climb. And this place is death for you, if any of my relatives find you here.

ROMEO: Love helped me to fly over the walls. No stone walls can keep love out. Love can do anything it wants. So your relatives can't stop me.

JULIET [*worried*]: But if they see you, they'll murder you.

ROMEO: There's more danger in your eyes for me than from twenty of their swords!

JULIET: But I don't want them to find you here!

ROMEO: The dark night will hide me from their eyes. And if I have your love, they can kill me. I prefer to die than to live without your love.

JULIET: You heard everything that I said tonight. You know how I feel about you. Do you love me too? I know that you'll say 'yes'. But if you love me, please don't play games with me. You make me very happy, but I'm not happy about this meeting tonight. It's happened too suddenly. My dear love, good night. I hope that by our next meeting our love can grow into a lovely flower.

ROMEO: Are you really going away without making me happy?

JULIET: How can I make you happy tonight?

ROMEO: By giving me your love in return for mine.

JULIET: I gave you my love before you asked for it. My love is as deep and as endless as the sea. [*listening*] I can hear a noise inside. Goodbye, my dear love! [*The Nurse calls from inside the house.*] I'm coming, Nurse! [*to Romeo*] Dear Montague, don't go away. Stay here for a little. I'll come back. [*She goes inside.*]

ROMEO: Oh, what a wonderful night! I'm afraid that all this is only a dream – it's not real.

[*Juliet comes back to her window, above.*]

'My love is as deep and as endless as the sea.'

JULIET: Just a few more words, dear Romeo, then it's really good night. If your love for me is true, I'll send somebody to you tomorrow. Give that person a message for me. Tell me the time and place that you'll marry me. Then I'll give you everything I have. I'll follow you all over the world.

NURSE [*from inside*]: Madam!

JULIET [*calling to the Nurse*]: I'm coming now! [*to Romeo*] But if you're not serious about me, I ask you ...

NURSE [*from inside*]: Madam!

JULIET [*to the Nurse*]: I'm just coming! [*to Romeo*] ... to go away and leave me to my pain. I'll send a message to you tomorrow. A thousand times good night! [*She goes inside.*]

ROMEO [*to himself*]: The night is a thousand times darker without your light. A lover runs to his love as fast as schoolboys run away from their lessons. But he walks away from his love as sadly as boys on their way to school.

[*Juliet comes back to the window again.*]

JULIET: Romeo! What time shall I send you the message?

ROMEO: Nine o'clock.

JULIET: All right. It seems like twenty years until then. I've forgotten why I called you back.

ROMEO: Then I'll stand here until you remember.

JULIET: And I'll still forget if you continue standing there. It's nearly morning. Good night, good night! It's so sad to leave you. [*She goes inside.*]

ROMEO: Sleep in peace, my love! Night has ended. The grey morning is bringing light to the clouds in the east. I'll go to Friar Laurence's house. I'll tell him about my good luck and ask for his help.

Scene 2 The garden of Friar Laurence's house

[*Friar Laurence comes in alone, carrying a bag.*]

FRIAR: Before the sun is high in the sky, I must fill this bag with plants. There are so many different plants in the world, and they *all* have a useful purpose. Sometimes even bad things can do good. [*holding up a flower*] Inside this little flower, there's poison but there's medicine too. If you smell the flower, you'll feel strong and healthy. But if you taste it, your heart will stop.

[*Romeo arrives.*]

ROMEO: Good morning, Father.★

FRIAR [*surprised*]: Who greets me in this friendly way so early? Young son, why aren't you in bed? Old people can't sleep easily, but young people can. You didn't go to bed last night, Romeo, did you?

ROMEO [*laughing*]: You're right. I was passing my time in a better way than sleeping.

FRIAR [*angrily*]: What! Have you been with Rosaline?

ROMEO [*surprised*]: With Rosaline, my dear Father? No. I've forgotten that name. It brought me only sadness and pain.

FRIAR: Good boy! But where *have* you been then?

ROMEO: I'll tell you before you ask me again. I was at my enemy's party, enjoying myself. Suddenly I got badly hurt, and I hurt somebody too. But you can help both of us. You can make everything better.

FRIAR: I don't understand you at all. Explain clearly.

ROMEO: Well, clearly, then ... I've fallen in love with the beautiful daughter of rich Capulet, and she's in love with me too. We want to get married. Please, agree to marry us today.

★Father: the usual way to greet a friar

FRIAR [*very surprised*]: But this is a great change! Have you so quickly forgotten Rosaline, your great love? I see that young men don't fall in love with their hearts, only with their eyes. How many tears did you cry for Rosaline? I can still hear your unhappy voice and see your sad face. Have you really changed your mind about her now?

ROMEO: You were often angry with me about my love for her.

FRIAR: Yes, because it wasn't true love. But I didn't want you to stop loving one woman and start loving another.

ROMEO: Don't be angry with me. My new love is very different from Rosaline. She loves me as much as I love her.

FRIAR: Oh, Rosaline knew that you weren't deeply in love with her. All right then, come with me. I'll help you for one reason only. Perhaps this marriage will end the terrible hate between your two families. Perhaps it will turn that hate into love.

ROMEO: Let's go! I'm in a great hurry!

FRIAR: It's wiser to go slowly. When people run too fast, they fall over.

[*Romeo and the Friar leave.*]

Scene 3 The town square in Verona

[*Benvolio and Mercutio arrive.*]

MERCUTIO: Where *is* Romeo? Didn't he go home last night?

BENVOLIO: Not to his father's house. I spoke to his servant.

MERCUTIO: That pale-faced, cold-hearted girl, that Rosaline, is still giving him trouble. He'll go crazy with love.

BENVOLIO: Tybalt, old Capulet's relative, has sent a letter to Romeo's father's house.

MERCUTIO: It's an invitation to fight, I'm sure!

BENVOLIO: Then Romeo will answer it.

MERCUTIO: But poor Romeo is already dead – killed by love. Will he really be able to fight Tybalt and win?

BENVOLIO: What's so special about Tybalt?
MERCUTIO: Well, he's an excellent swordsman. He's like a professional fighter.

[*Romeo arrives, looking very happy.*]

ROMEO: Good morning to you both.
MERCUTIO: Good morning, Signor Romeo. You escaped from us very cleverly last night.
ROMEO: I'm sorry, my dear Mercutio. I had some very important business. But I'm sorry that I acted rudely.
MERCUTIO: Well, you're very friendly now. You're like the real Romeo again – the old friend that we know. Isn't this better than being sad about love?
ROMEO [*laughing*]: Here comes a strange-looking person!

[*The Nurse, dressed in bright clothes, arrives with Peter.*]

MERCUTIO [*laughing too and dancing round the Nurse*]: Two people! A man and a woman!
NURSE [*trying to get away from Mercutio*]: Good morning, gentlemen. Can you tell me where I can find young Romeo?
ROMEO: Yes, I can tell you. That's my name.
NURSE: If you *are* Romeo, I'd like to speak to you alone.
BENVOLIO [*to Mercutio*]: Perhaps she's going to ask him to dinner.

[*Mercutio laughs loudly.*]

MERCUTIO: Romeo, are you coming to your father's house?
ROMEO: I'll meet you there later.
MERCUTIO [*kissing the Nurse's hand*]: Goodbye, old lady.

[*Mercutio and Benvolio leave.*]

NURSE: Who was that rude young man?
ROMEO: A gentleman, Nurse, who loves to hear himself talk. He says more things in a minute than he'll do in a month.

NURSE: Rude boy! [*turning to Peter*] Why did you just stand there? Why didn't you stop him making fun of me?

PETER [*laughing*]: I didn't notice him making fun of you.

NURSE: I'm so angry. What a rude boy! [*taking Romeo to one side*] Now, sir, my young lady asked me to find you. But first, I want to say something. If you're only playing with her feelings, that's wrong of you. My lady's very young.

ROMEO: Oh no, Nurse, I'm very serious. Please give my best greetings to your lady. I promise . . .

NURSE: Oh, good, I'll tell her. She'll be a very happy woman!

ROMEO: But what are you going to tell her, Nurse? You're not listening to me.

NURSE: I'll tell her, sir, that you promise to marry her, like a true gentleman.

ROMEO: Good. Tell her to come to Friar Laurence's house this afternoon. And there she and I can get married. [*giving the Nurse some money*] Here, take this.

NURSE: Oh no, really, sir. I don't want any money.

ROMEO: Go on, take it.

NURSE [*taking the money*]: This afternoon, sir? She'll be there.

ROMEO: And wait, dear Nurse, behind the church wall. My servant will come to you in an hour and bring you a rope. I'll use it to climb up secretly to my lady's bedroom tonight. Goodbye. Give my best greetings to your lady.

NURSE: Thank you, sir! Listen . . .

ROMEO: What do you want to tell me, dear Nurse?

NURSE: Well, sir, my lady is the sweetest lady. I remember when she was a little girl . . . Oh, there's a gentleman in town called Paris. He would very much like to marry her, but she hates him. I make her angry sometimes. I tell her that Paris is a fine man.

ROMEO: Give my best greetings to your lady. [*He leaves.*]

NURSE: Yes, a thousand times. Peter!

PETER: Coming!
NURSE: Walk in front of me, and hurry up!

[*The Nurse and Peter leave.*]

Scene 4 Juliet's bedroom

[*Juliet comes in.*]

JULIET: I sent Nurse to find Romeo at nine o'clock. She promised to return in half an hour. Oh, she's so slow! The messengers of love have to travel quickly! It's midday now, three long hours and she still hasn't come back. She's old. She doesn't have the feelings and the warm blood of a young person. She doesn't do things quickly, but moves slowly and heavily. [*The Nurse and Peter come in.*] Oh, sweet Nurse, what news? Did you meet Romeo? Send Peter away.

NURSE: Peter, go and wait by the gate.

[*Peter goes out.*]

JULIET: Now, dear sweet Nurse ... Oh, why do you look so sad? If you have bad news, tell me kindly. If it's good news, then don't look so unhappy.

NURSE [*sitting down*]: I'm tired. Leave me alone for a time. All my body aches! I've walked a long way!

JULIET: Come on, tell me, speak. Dear, dear Nurse, speak!

NURSE: What's your hurry? Can't you wait for a few minutes? Don't you see that I need to rest?

JULIET: Is your news good or bad? Just answer that and I'll be happy. Is it good or bad?

NURSE: Well ... Romeo's face is more handsome than other men's faces. You can't compare his body with other men's bodies – his is better. He's a very nice and polite young man. Have you had dinner yet?

JULIET: No, no. But I knew all these things before. What did he say about our marriage? What about that?

NURSE: I've got a terrible headache! My head is breaking into twenty pieces. My back's hurting too – oh, my back, my back! Why did you send me out? I nearly died from that long walk!

JULIET [*trying to be patient*]: I'm really sorry you're not feeling well. Sweet, sweet Nurse, tell me, what did my love say?

NURSE: Your love says, like an honest gentleman, and a kind and polite one ... Where's your mother?

JULIET [*angry now*]: My mother? Here, at home. Where do you think she is? What a strange answer! 'Your love says, like an honest gentleman, "Where's your mother?"'

NURSE: Dear lady, why are you so angry? Is this all the thanks I get? Is this going to help my aching body? In future, you can take your own messages!

JULIET [*very patiently*]: What did Romeo say?

NURSE: Have you got permission to go to church today?

JULIET: I have.

NURSE: Then hurry to Friar Laurence's house. Your husband is waiting for you there. Now your face is turning red! I have to go a different way and get a rope. Your love is going to use it to climb up to your room after dark. I'm doing all this hard work just to please you. Now I'm going to have my dinner. Go quickly to Friar Laurence.

JULIET: I'll hurry. What wonderful luck! Dear Nurse, goodbye.

[*Juliet and the Nurse go out.*]

Scene 5 A room in Friar Laurence's house

[*Friar Laurence and Romeo come in.*]

FRIAR [*worried*]: I hope that this marriage won't result in any trouble for us.

ROMEO: I hope not too. But if sadness follows, it can't take away the happiness of one short minute with Juliet. If you join our hands in marriage, death can't hurt us. If I can call her mine, that's enough for me.

FRIAR: These strong feelings of love don't bring happiness. They burn, and then they die. Don't love so strongly. Then your love will be a long one. [*looking up and seeing Juliet*] Here comes the lady. How fast and lightly she runs!

[*Juliet comes running in. She kisses Romeo.*]

JULIET: Good evening, Father.

FRIAR: Good evening.

ROMEO: Ah, Juliet, are you filled with happiness as I am? Speak to me with your sweet, musical voice.

JULIET: I can't describe how happy I am!

FRIAR: Come with me. This won't take long. I'm not going to leave you two alone until you're married.

[*Romeo, Juliet and the Friar go out.*]

Act 3 Murder and Banishment

Scene 1 *The town square in Verona*

[*Mercutio and Benvolio arrive. Abram and Balthasar follow.*]

BENVOLIO: Please, dear Mercutio, let's go home. It's very hot and the Capulets are in town. If we meet them, we'll get into a fight. This heat is making everybody crazy.

MERCUTIO: You're the kind of person who likes starting fights.

BENVOLIO [*surprised*]: Me? Am I really?

MERCUTIO: Yes. You're always looking for trouble. And now you're telling *me* not to get into a fight.

[*Tybalt arrives from the other side. Sampson and Gregory follow.*]

BENVOLIO: Oh no! Here come the Capulets.

MERCUTIO: Oh, good!

TYBALT [*to Sampson and Gregory*]: Stay close behind me – I'm going to speak to these Montagues. Good evening, gentlemen. Can I talk to you?

MERCUTIO: You only want to *talk* to us? Don't you want to fight us too?

TYBALT: You'll find me ready for that, sir, if you make me angry. Mercutio, you're a great friend of Romeo's.

MERCUTIO: That's right. Is that a problem? [*taking out his sword*] Here's my sword. Do you want to feel its point?

BENVOLIO [*trying to keep the peace*]: We're talking in a very open place. Let's go somewhere private, or discuss things calmly. Everybody is looking at us.

MERCUTIO: Fine. They can look. But I'm not leaving here.

[*Romeo arrives.*]

TYBALT [*to Mercutio*]: Well, I'm not interested in fighting you, sir. Here comes the man I'm interested in. [*standing in Romeo's way*] Romeo, my heart fills with hate when I see you.

ROMEO [*calmly*]: I have a very good reason to love you, Tybalt. So I'm not going to get angry about the way you've greeted me. You don't know who I am. Goodbye. [*He starts to walk away.*]

TYBALT [*following him*]: Boy, you've acted badly towards me. You're not going to escape now. Turn and take out your sword.

ROMEO [*turning*]: I've never done anything wrong to you. I love you better than you can imagine. I love your name as much as mine. So please, dear Capulet, don't continue trying to make me angry. [*He starts to walk away again.*]

MERCUTIO [*angrily to Romeo*]: Why are you being so weak? Do you want Tybalt to win? [*taking out his sword*] Tybalt, come over here!

TYBALT [*going towards Mercutio*]: What do you want with me?
MERCUTIO: To fight you. Take your sword out before I kill you.
TYBALT: I'm ready for you. [*He takes out his sword.*]
ROMEO: Dear Mercutio, put your sword away.
MERCUTIO [*to Tybalt*]: Let's see how well you can use a sword!

[*Mercutio and Tybalt start to fight.*]

ROMEO: Take your sword out, Benvolio! Help me stop this fight! Please, gentlemen, put your swords away. The Prince has ordered you not to fight in the streets of Verona. Stop, Tybalt! Stop, Mercutio!

[*Romeo steps between Tybalt and Mercutio. He puts up his arms to stop the fight. Tybalt pushes his sword into Mercutio.*]

SAMPSON: Run away quickly, Tybalt!

[*Tybalt runs away with Sampson and Gregory.*]

MERCUTIO [*falling down*]: I'm hurt! A curse on both your families! I'm dying. Has Tybalt escaped? Isn't he hurt?
BENVOLIO [*holding Mercutio*]: Are you really hurt?
MERCUTIO: Yes, yes, it's only a small cut, but it's enough. [*to Abram*] Go and get a doctor.

[*Abram hurries away.*]

ROMEO: Be brave, man. It can't be a very deep cut.
MERCUTIO: No, it isn't very deep, or very wide. But it's enough to kill me. Ask for me tomorrow, and you'll find me in my grave. A curse on both your families! [*to Romeo*] Why did you come between us? I was hurt when you put your arms up.
ROMEO [*sadly*]: I was only trying to help.
MERCUTIO: Help me into a house, Benvolio. A curse on both your families! They have killed me.

'Please, gentlemen, put your swords away.'

[*Benvolio takes Mercutio away.*]

ROMEO: Mercutio, the Prince's close relative and my dear friend, is seriously hurt because of me. Oh, sweet Juliet, I saw your lovely face and acted like a woman!

[*Benvolio returns.*]

BENVOLIO: Oh Romeo, Romeo, brave Mercutio is dead!
ROMEO: Sad things have happened today but they're only the beginning. More troubles are going to follow.

[*Tybalt returns.*]

BENVOLIO: Here comes the angry Tybalt back again.
ROMEO: Tybalt is alive, and Mercutio is dead! I'm not going to hold myself back now. Tybalt, Mercutio is waiting for you to join him in death. One of us, or both of us, must go with him.
TYBALT: You were his friend, you stupid boy. *You* go with him!
ROMEO: Let's fight! We'll see what happens!

[*They fight. Romeo kills Tybalt. Tybalt falls down.*]

BENVOLIO: Tybalt is dead! The townspeople are coming! Run, Romeo! Don't just stand there looking surprised. If they catch you, the Prince will order your death. Go, run!
ROMEO: Oh, what have I done!
BENVOLIO: What are you waiting for? Run away!

[*Romeo runs away and the townspeople arrive.*]

TOWNSPEOPLE: Which way did Mercutio's murderer run? Which way did that murderer Tybalt go?
BENVOLIO [*pointing to Tybalt's body*]: Tybalt is lying there.

[*The Prince, Lord Montague, Lord Capulet and their wives arrive.*]

PRINCE: Who began this terrible fight?

BENVOLIO: Oh, noble Prince, I can tell you everything. There's Tybalt, the man who killed your brave relative, Mercutio. He's lying there dead. He was killed by young Romeo.

LADY CAPULET [*falling on Tybalt's dead body and crying*]: Tybalt! Oh, my brother's child! Oh, Prince! Husband! Tybalt is dead! Prince, a Montague killed Tybalt. Take the life of a Montague in return for his death. Oh, Tybalt, Tybalt!

PRINCE: Benvolio, who started this terrible fight?

BENVOLIO: Tybalt. Romeo spoke to him very calmly and asked him not to fight. But Tybalt was angry and didn't want to listen. He started fighting Mercutio. Romeo put up his arms to stop them fighting. Tybalt pushed his sword into Mercutio under Romeo's arm. Tybalt ran away, but later he returned. Romeo, crazy from Mercutio's death, started to fight Tybalt. Before I could stop the fight, Romeo killed Tybalt. Then he ran away.

LADY CAPULET: Benvolio is a relative of the Montagues. He's lying. Romeo killed Tybalt, so Romeo must die too.

PRINCE [*sadly*]: Tybalt killed Mercutio. Romeo killed Tybalt. Whose turn is it to die now?

LORD MONTAGUE: Not Romeo's, Prince. He was Mercutio's friend. Tybalt killed Mercutio. His punishment by law is death. So Romeo killed him.

PRINCE: And for that crime, I am going to banish him from Verona. Mercutio was my relative. I have lost him because of your stupid fighting. [*to Lord and Lady Montague*] It is no use crying. I am not going to listen to excuses and I am not going to change my mind. Romeo must leave now. If we find him in Verona after this, he must die. [*turning to the townspeople, and pointing to Tybalt's body*] Take this body away.

[*Some people pick up Tybalt's body and leave. Everybody follows.*]

Scene 2 Juliet's bedroom

[*Juliet comes in, alone.*]

JULIET: Hurry, sun, go down! Night is the time for lovers. Come, night, come, Romeo. You are like the bright day to me. Today is passing so slowly. I am as excited as a child with new party clothes. [*The Nurse comes in, looking very worried and unhappy, with the rope.*] Oh, here comes my nurse, with news. What is it, Nurse? Have you brought the rope?

NURSE [*sadly*]: Yes, yes, here's the rope. [*She throws it down.*]

JULIET [*worried*]: What's happened? What's the matter?

NURSE [*crying*]: He's dead, he's dead, he's dead! Everything is finished for us, lady! Oh, what a sad day! He's dead, he's dead! Oh, Romeo! Who could imagine this terrible thing!

JULIET: Has Romeo killed himself? Give me a quick answer. If he *is* dead, just say 'yes'. If not, 'no'.

NURSE: I saw his dead body, I saw it with my own eyes. It was pale, all pale and covered in blood.

JULIET: Now my heart will break! If Romeo is dead, I want to die too!

NURSE: Oh, Tybalt, Tybalt, my best friend! Oh, dear Tybalt! I'm still alive and you're dead!

JULIET: What's this? Are Tybalt and Romeo both dead? My dearest cousin and my dearer husband?

NURSE: Tybalt is dead and the Prince has banished Romeo from Verona.

JULIET: Did Romeo kill Tybalt?

NURSE: Yes, yes! Oh, sad day, yes! A curse on Romeo!

JULIET: Don't talk about Romeo like that!

NURSE: Are you defending your cousin's murderer?

JULIET: Do you want me to say bad things about my husband? [*to herself*] Oh, my poor Romeo! Who will say kind things about you if I, your wife of three hours, cannot? But why did you kill my cousin? Or did my cousin want to kill you? [*thinking*] Romeo is alive. That's a reason to be happy. So why am I crying? [*turning to the Nurse*] So Romeo is banished. That word 'banished' is more terrible than the death of ten thousand Tybalts. Where are my father and mother?

NURSE: Crying by Tybalt's body. Do you want to go to them? I'll take you there.

JULIET: No. They can wash his body with their tears. When their tears are dry, I'll still cry about Romeo's banishment. Pick up the rope. Romeo planned to use it tonight as a pathway to my bed. But that's not going to happen now.

NURSE: Hurry to your room. I'll go and find Romeo. I know where he is. He's at Friar Laurence's house.

JULIET: Oh, find him! [*giving the Nurse a ring*] Give this ring to my true love. Tell him to come and say goodbye to me for the last time.

[*Juliet and the Nurse go out.*]

Scene 3 A room in Friar Laurence's house

[*Friar Laurence comes in.*]

FRIAR [*calling*]: Come out, Romeo. Don't be afraid.

[*Romeo comes in.*]

ROMEO: What news, Friar? What are the Prince's orders? What new troubles are coming to me?

FRIAR: You're always thinking about problems.

ROMEO: Has the Prince ordered my death?

FRIAR: No, it isn't as bad as that. He's ordered your banishment.

ROMEO: Banishment? Be kind, say 'death'. Banishment is more terrible than death.

FRIAR: He has banished you from Verona. But don't lose hope. The world is a big place.

ROMEO: There *is* no world outside the walls of Verona.

FRIAR: You're very ungrateful! The usual punishment for your crime is death. But the kind Prince has changed that black word 'death' into 'banishment'. That's a great kindness, and you can't see it.

ROMEO: It *isn't* a kindness. All my happiness is here. Every cat and dog can live here happily and look at Juliet. But I can't because the Prince has banished me. Don't you have any poison to kill me with? How can you, a religious man and my friend, hurt me so much?

FRIAR: You silly boy, listen to me.

ROMEO: Don't talk about things that you can't understand. You don't know how I feel. I'm in love with Juliet, I got married a few hours ago, Tybalt is dead, the Prince has banished me ... [*He lies down on the floor, crying.*]

[*Somebody knocks at the door.*]

FRIAR [*afraid*]: Get up. There's somebody at the door. Hide yourself, Romeo.

ROMEO: No. Why?

[*The knocking gets louder.*]

FRIAR [*to the person at the door*]: Who's there? [*trying to pull Romeo up*] Romeo, get up. They'll take you prisoner. [*to the person at the door*] Wait! [*to Romeo*] Get up! [*more knocking*] Go and hide in my office. [*to the person at the door*] I'm coming! [*to Romeo*] Don't act in this stupid way! [*to the person at the door*] I'm just coming! What do you want?

NURSE: Let me in, and I'll tell you. I've come from Lady Juliet.

FRIAR: Welcome, then.

[*The Friar opens the door and the Nurse comes in.*]

NURSE: Oh, tell me, Friar, where's my lady's husband? Where's Romeo?

FRIAR [*pointing to Romeo*]: There, on the floor, crying.

NURSE: Oh, Juliet is just the same, exactly the same! What a terrible thing. [*to Romeo*] Get up, if you're a man! Think about Juliet and get up! Why are you acting in this silly way?

[*Romeo gets up.*]

ROMEO: Nurse . . .

NURSE: Ah, sir! Ah, sir! Death is the end of everything!

ROMEO: Did you say something about Juliet? How is she? I've killed her cousin and destroyed our happiness. Where is she? *How* is she? What does she say about our love?

NURSE: She doesn't say anything, sir. She cries and cries. She falls down on her bed, then gets up. She calls out Tybalt's name, and then Romeo's, and then falls again.

ROMEO: My name is hateful to me. I'm going to kill myself. [*He takes out a knife. The Nurse takes the knife away quickly.*]

FRIAR: Stop! Are you a man? You look like a man, but you're crying like a woman and you're acting like a wild animal. You've already killed Tybalt. Are you going to kill yourself now, and Juliet too? Stop acting like this! Your Juliet is alive. That's a reason to be happy! Tybalt wanted to kill you, but you killed Tybalt. That's another reason to be happy. The Prince has changed death into banishment. That's *another* reason to be happy! So be grateful for your good luck. Go to Juliet, as we decided before. Climb up to her room tonight. Early in the morning you must leave for Mantua.* Later, we'll tell everyone about your marriage and ask the Prince to forgive you. Then you can come back to Verona, happier than you are now. You go first, Nurse. Give my best greetings to Juliet. Tell her to send the servants to bed early tonight. Romeo is coming.

---

*Mantua: a town about forty kilometres from Verona

NURSE: Oh, how clever you are! [*to Romeo*] I'll tell my lady that you're coming. [*She starts to leave, then turns back and takes out Juliet's ring.*] Here, sir, she asked me to give you this ring. Hurry – it's getting very late. [*She goes out.*]

ROMEO: I feel much happier now!

FRIAR: Go now. You must leave Verona before daylight tomorrow morning, before the city guards see you. Go to Mantua. I'll find your servant and give messages to him. He'll bring you all the good news from here. Goodbye.

ROMEO [*giving his hand to the Friar*]: I'm very sorry to leave you. But happiness is waiting for me. Goodbye.

[*Romeo and the Friar go out.*]

Scene 4 A room in the Capulets' house

[*Lord and Lady Capulet come in with Paris.*]

LORD CAPULET: Many sad things have happened, sir. We haven't had time to talk to our daughter about marriage. You must understand that she loved her cousin Tybalt very much. I did too. Well, everything ends in death. It's late. She won't come down tonight. It's time for us to go to bed.

PARIS [*to Lady Capulet*]: Good night, Madam. Give my best greetings to your daughter.

LADY CAPULET: I will. I'll talk to her early in the morning. She's shut up in her room tonight, full of her great sadness.

[*Paris starts to leave but Lord Capulet calls him back.*]

LORD CAPULET: Sir Paris, I'm going to make you an offer of my child's love. I'm sure that she'll listen to me in everything. Wife, talk to Juliet before you go to bed. Tell her about Paris's love. Tell her – are you listening to me? – that on Wednesday ... But wait! What day is it today?

PARIS: Monday.

LORD CAPULET: Monday! Well, Wednesday is too soon. Let's say Thursday. Tell her that on Thursday, this noble gentleman will marry her. [to Paris] Will you be ready by then? Do you mind this hurry? It won't be a big wedding, only one or two guests. Tybalt has just died so we can't have a big party. But what do you think about Thursday?

PARIS: It's a long time until Thursday!

LORD CAPULET: Well, go home now. [to Lady Capulet] Talk to Juliet before you go to bed. Prepare her for this wedding day. [to Paris] Good night, sir.

[Paris goes out, and Lord and Lady Capulet follow.]

Scene 5 Juliet's bedroom

[Romeo and Juliet stand by the window.]

JULIET: Do you really have to go? It's still night.

ROMEO: No, morning is coming. See, my love, the clouds of night are moving away in the east. The stars have disappeared and there's daylight over the mountain tops. If I want to live, I have to leave now. If I stay here, I'll die.

JULIET: That light isn't daylight. I'm sure about that! Please stay. You don't have to go yet.

ROMEO: Then they can take me prisoner and kill me. I'm happy, if you are. That grey light isn't the light of morning – it's moonlight. I prefer to stay here with you than to go. Welcome, death! Let's talk, my love. It isn't daylight yet.

JULIET [worried]: Yes, it is, it is! Hurry away from here – go! It's getting lighter and lighter.

ROMEO: It's getting lighter, but our troubles are getting darker.

[The Nurse hurries in.]

NURSE: Madam!

JULIET: Yes, Nurse?

NURSE: Your mother's coming to your room. It's daylight now. Be careful. [*She goes out.*]

JULIET [*opening the window*]: Daylight comes in through this window but Romeo, the light of my life, goes out.

ROMEO: Goodbye! Give me a kiss and I'll climb down. [*He climbs through the window.*]

JULIET: Have you gone, my love, my friend, my husband? I want to hear from you every hour of every day.

ROMEO: Goodbye! I'll send you messages as often as I can.

JULIET: Oh, do you think we'll ever meet again?

ROMEO: Of course we will. One day in the future we'll talk about these troubles and laugh.

JULIET: Oh, I'm imagining terrible things. I see you looking like a dead man in a grave. You're very pale.

ROMEO: And you're pale too, my love. We look pale because we're so sad. Goodbye, goodbye! [*He leaves.*]

JULIET: Oh, how unlucky we are!

[*Juliet goes away from the window. Lady Capulet comes in.*]

LADY CAPULET: Hello, daughter! Are you up?

JULIET [*to herself*]: It's my mother. Is she going to bed very late, or has she got up very early? Why has she come here?

LADY CAPULET: How are you, Juliet?

JULIET: Madam, I'm not very well.

LADY CAPULET: Are you still crying about Tybalt's death? Do you want to wash him out of his grave with tears? You can't bring him back to life. So stop crying.

JULIET: I loved him very much, and now I've lost him.

LADY CAPULET: Perhaps you're crying because his murderer is still alive.

JULIET: What murderer, Madam?

LADY CAPULET: Romeo.

JULIET [*to herself*]: Romeo isn't a murderer! [*to Lady Capulet*] Yes, nobody gives my heart more pain than Romeo.

LADY CAPULET: Don't cry. I'll send a message to a man in Mantua. Romeo is living there now. I'll tell him to poison Romeo. Then he'll be dead, and you'll be happy. [*Juliet looks pale and frightened.*] But I've brought you some good news.

JULIET: Good news is always welcome in sad times. What is it?

LADY CAPULET: You have a wise father, child. He knows how unhappy you are. So he's preparing a very happy day for you.

JULIET [*worried*]: Really, Madam? What day is that?

LADY CAPULET: Early on Thursday morning, the noble young Paris will marry you at St Peter's Church.

JULIET [*surprised and very angry*]: No, he won't! Please tell my father, Madam, that I'm not ready for marriage. And when I *am* ready, I prefer to marry Romeo than Paris. And you know that I hate Romeo. This is terrible news!

LADY CAPULET [*coldly*]: Here comes your father. Tell him yourself. See what kind of answer he gives you!

[*Lord Capulet and the Nurse come in.*]

LORD CAPULET: How are you, girl? Not still crying about Tybalt? Well, wife? Did you tell her about our decision?

LADY CAPULET: Yes, I did. But the silly girl isn't happy about our plans for her.

LORD CAPULET [*surprised and angry*]: What do you mean? I don't understand you, wife. Isn't she grateful to us? We've found a very fine husband for her. Isn't she pleased?

JULIET: I'm not pleased, but I *am* thankful. I can't be pleased about something hateful. But I *can* be thankful for something that is done for love – even a hateful thing.

LORD CAPULET [*very angry now*]: What's all this? 'Pleased' and 'I'm thankful' and 'I'm not thankful' and 'I'm not pleased'? Listen, my fine lady, get yourself ready to go with Paris to St Peter's Church on Thursday. Or I'll pull you there!

LADY CAPULET [*to Capulet*]: Stop, stop! Are you crazy?

JULIET [*getting down on her knees and crying*]: Father, please be patient. Please listen to me!

LORD CAPULET: You ungrateful girl! I'm telling you, get to church on Thursday or never look me in the face again! Wife, we were very lucky to have one child. That's what we thought. But I see now that this child is a curse for us.

NURSE: Don't be angry with her, sir.

LORD CAPULET: And why not? You're a stupid old woman! Be quiet!

LADY CAPULET: Don't be so angry.

LORD CAPULET: It makes me crazy! Every hour of every day, I've worked hard to find a good husband for her. Now I've found a fine young gentleman from a noble family. [*to Juliet*] Well, if you don't marry him, I'll never forgive you! You can't stay here in my house. I'm not joking! If you want to continue as my daughter, I'll give you to Paris. If not, then die in the streets. I'll never speak to you again, or give you any money or help. Think about it! [*He goes out.*]

JULIET [*turning to Lady Capulet*]: Is there no pity in heaven? Oh, my sweet mother, please don't throw me out. Stop this marriage only for a month, or even a week. Or put my wedding-bed in the dark vault where Tybalt's body lies.

LADY CAPULET [*coldly*]: Don't talk to me. I'm not going to say anything to help you. [*She goes out.*]

JULIET [*turning to the Nurse*]: Oh, Nurse, how can we stop this terrible marriage? Please help me. Say something kind to me.

NURSE: All right, then. The Prince has banished Romeo and Romeo can't return. So I think you should marry Paris. Oh, he's a fine gentleman. I'm sure you'll be happy in this second marriage. It's better than your first. And even if it isn't, your first marriage has ended. Romeo is of no use to you now.

JULIET [*very quietly*]: Do you really mean that?

NURSE: Yes, I do.

JULIET [*thinking for a time before speaking*]: Well, thank you very much. I feel much better now. Tell my mother that I've gone to see Friar Laurence.

NURSE: I will. You're doing a wise thing. [*The Nurse goes out.*]

JULIET: The bad old woman! She's said a thousand good things about Romeo in the past. I'll never tell her my secrets again. I'll go and see Friar Laurence. Perhaps he'll have a plan to help me. If not, I can kill myself.

Act 4   The Sweetest Flower

Scene 1   *A room in Friar Laurence's house*

[*Friar Laurence and Paris come in.*]

FRIAR [*worried*]: On Thursday, sir? That's not much time.

PARIS: It's her father's decision. But I'm happy about it too.

FRIAR: And you don't know how the lady feels about the marriage? That's very unusual. I don't like it.

PARIS: She's still crying all the time about Tybalt's death. I haven't talked to her very much about love. In her father's opinion, her great sadness is dangerous for her health. If our wedding takes place quickly, she'll forget her sadness.

FRIAR [*to himself*]: There's a very good reason *not* to hurry. [*to Paris*] Look, here comes the lady.

[*Juliet comes in.*]

PARIS: This is a happy meeting, my lady and my wife.

JULIET [*quietly*]: I am not your wife yet, sir.

PARIS: But we're going to be married on Thursday. Have you come to see the Friar?

JULIET: Yes, I have. [*to Friar Laurence*] Do you have time to see me now, Father? Or shall I come and see you this evening?

FRIAR: No, I have time now. [*to Paris*] Sir, please excuse us. The lady and I must talk alone.

PARIS: Yes, of course. [*to Juliet*] Juliet, I'll come for you early on Thursday morning. Until then, goodbye, and keep this kiss. [*He kisses her and goes out.*]

JULIET [*to the Friar*]: Oh, close the door! Then come and cry with me. There's no more hope, or help!

FRIAR [*closing the door*]: Oh, Juliet, I know about your problems already. But I don't know how to solve them. I hear that you have to marry this gentleman on Thursday.

JULIET: Don't tell me that you already know this, Friar. Tell me that you can stop this marriage. If you can't help me, I'll kill myself with this knife. [*taking out a knife*] You're a wise man. So tell me what to do. Why are you so silent? If you can't think of a good plan, I'll die.

FRIAR [*taking the knife from her*]: Wait, daughter. I can see a kind of hope, but it's a little dangerous. But you're very brave. You prefer to die than to marry Paris. So perhaps you're brave enough to do this thing.

JULIET: Tell me to jump from a great height. Tell me to go to a place with thieves, or wild animals. Put me in a grave with a dead man. I'm frightened of all these things, but I'll do them.

FRIAR: All right, then. Go home, be happy, agree to marry Paris. [*Juliet looks surprised.*] It's Wednesday tomorrow. Tomorrow night make sure that you go to bed alone. Tell Nurse not to stay with you. [*taking out a small bottle and giving it to her*] Then take this bottle and drink the medicine. Soon, a cold, sleepy feeling will run through your body. Your face will turn white, your eyes will close and your body will become cold. Everybody will think that you're dead. You'll be like that for forty-two hours, and then you'll wake up. When Paris comes for you on Thursday morning, he'll find you dead in bed. Your

'Take this bottle and drink the medicine.'

family will dress you in your best clothes. They'll carry your body to the vault where all the dead Capulets lie. I'll send a letter to Romeo in Mantua and ask him to come. He and I will go to the vault and wait there until you wake up. Then he'll take you back to Mantua with him. So you won't have to marry Paris. But are you brave enough to do this?

JULIET [*putting out her hand*]: Give me the bottle!

FRIAR [*giving her the bottle*]: All right, here it is. Go now. Be strong, and good luck. I'll send a friar to Mantua with a letter for Romeo.

JULIET: Love, help me do this. Make me strong. Goodbye, dear Father.

[*Juliet and the Friar go out.*]

Scene 2 A room in the Capulets' house

[*Lord and Lady Capulet come in with the Nurse and Peter.*]

LORD CAPULET [*to Peter*]: Go and invite all the guests on this list. Then find twenty excellent cooks. [*Peter goes out.*] [*to the Nurse*] Has my daughter gone to see Friar Laurence?

NURSE: Yes, she has.

LORD CAPULET: Well, I hope she listens to him. Perhaps she'll become more sensible. She's a very silly girl.

[*Juliet comes in.*]

NURSE: Here she comes. She looks very happy.

LORD CAPULET [*to Juliet*]: Where have you been, girl?

JULIET: I'm very sorry, Father. Friar Laurence has told me to ask for your forgiveness. [*getting down on her knees*] Please forgive me! I'll do everything you want.

LORD CAPULET [*very happy*]: I'll send for Paris immediately! I can't wait for Thursday. We'll have this wedding tomorrow.

JULIET: I met noble young Paris at Friar Laurence's house. I had a friendly conversation with him.
LORD CAPULET: Excellent! I'm very happy about that. Get up. [*giving Juliet his hand and helping her up*] Now everything is all right again. Yes, I'll send for Paris.
JULIET: Nurse, please come to my room with me. Help me choose some nice clothes for tomorrow.
LADY CAPULET: Wait! Thursday is soon enough.
LORD CAPULET: Go, Nurse, go with her. We'll have the wedding tomorrow.

[*Juliet and the Nurse go out.*]

LADY CAPULET: We won't have time to finish our preparations. It's nearly night.
LORD CAPULET: I'll start getting things ready. Everything will be fine, I promise you, wife. Go and help Juliet choose her wedding clothes. I'm not going to go to bed tonight. I'll walk to Paris's house and tell him the good news.

[*Lord and Lady Capulet go out.*]

Scene 3   Juliet's bedroom

[*Juliet and the Nurse come in.*]

JULIET: Yes, that dress is the best one. But now, dear Nurse, please leave me. I want to be alone tonight.

[*Lady Capulet comes in.*]

LADY CAPULET: Are you busy? Do you need my help?
JULIET: No, Madam. I've chosen everything that I need for tomorrow. So please leave me alone now. Nurse can stay with you tonight. I'm sure you are all very busy with this sudden wedding.

LADY CAPULET: Goodnight. Sleep well. You need to rest.

[*Lady Capulet and the Nurse go out.*]

JULIET [*sitting on her bed*]: Goodbye! I don't know if we'll ever meet again. There's a cold fear running through my body. I'll call them back again. [*calling*] Nurse! No, I must do this terrible thing alone. [*taking out the bottle*] Perhaps the Friar has given me poison. No, no, he's a good man. Perhaps I'll wake up in the vault before Romeo comes? There's no fresh air in that dark place. I'll die, or I'll go crazy with fear. The bodies of the dead Capulets have been there for hundreds of years. Tybalt's body is lying there too. Oh, look! I think I can see Tybalt now. He's looking for Romeo. Stop, Tybalt! Romeo, Romeo! I drink to you! [*She drinks the medicine and falls on her bed.*]

Scene 4 A room in the Capulets' house

[*Lord and Lady Capulet come in with the Nurse.*]

LORD CAPULET: Hurry, hurry! There's not much time. It's three o'clock in the morning. [*to the Nurse*] Go and help get the food ready in the kitchen.

[*Lady Capulet and the Nurse go out. Peter comes in, carrying kitchen equipment.*]

LORD CAPULET: What have you got there?
PETER: Things for the cook, sir. I don't know what they are.
LORD CAPULET: Hurry, hurry! Go and get dry wood for the fire. [*Peter goes out.*] It's nearly day. Paris will be here soon. He's going to bring some music with him. [*Music plays.*] Here he comes. Nurse! Wife! Nurse! [*The Nurse comes in.*] Go and wake Juliet up. Get her ready. I'll go and talk to Paris. Hurry! Paris is here already. Hurry, I say!

[*Lord Capulet goes out. The Nurse follows.*]

Scene 5 Juliet's bedroom

[*The Nurse goes to Juliet's bed.*]

NURSE: Juliet! My lady! Come on, get up, don't be so lazy! Well, sleep then. [*laughing*] You won't get much sleep tonight. [*to herself*] She's in a very deep sleep. But I have to wake her up. [*to Juliet*] Madam, Madam, Madam! All right, Paris can find you in bed. [*looking closely at Juliet*] What's this? Did you sleep in your clothes last night? Lady, Lady! [*She shakes Juliet and starts to scream.*] Help, help! My lady's dead! Sir! Madam! Come quickly!

[*Lady Capulet hurries in.*]

LADY CAPULET: Why are you making all this noise?
NURSE [*pointing to Juliet*]: Look, look!
LADY CAPULET [*looking at Juliet and starting to scream too*]: Oh, my child, my life! Wake up, or I'll die too!

[*Lord Capulet hurries in.*]

LORD CAPULET: Bring Juliet down. Her husband has come.
NURSE [*crying*]: She's dead, she's dead!
LADY CAPULET [*crying too*]: Yes, she's dead! It's terrible!
LORD CAPULET [*feeling Juliet's body*]: She's cold. Death lies on her like early snow on the sweetest flower in the field.
NURSE: Oh, what a terrible day!

[*Friar Laurence and Paris come in.*]

FRIAR: Come, is Juliet ready to go to church?
LORD CAPULET: She's ready to go there, but never to return. [*to Paris*] Oh, my son, your wife is dead. [*showing him Juliet's body*] Death has taken her.
PARIS: I've waited for this day for a long time. But now – it's terrible!

LADY CAPULET: It's the worst day that has ever happened. I had only one child – one child to make me happy. And now death has taken her from me.

NURSE: Oh sad, unhappy day!

PARIS: I've lost everything. Hateful death has taken my love – my love and my life – from me.

LORD CAPULET: Oh, my child, my child! She's dead – my dear child is dead – and all my happiness has died with her!

FRIAR: Be quiet, please. All this noise doesn't help things. You couldn't keep this lovely child with you here on earth. But she's very happy in heaven, so don't cry for her. Dress her in her best clothes and carry her dead body to church.

LORD CAPULET: Everything has changed. We have to take off our bright wedding clothes and put on black ones. Our happy wedding music must change to the sad music of death.

FRIAR: Sir, and Madam, go and get ready – and you too, Paris. Prepare to follow this lovely young girl to her grave. You have made the heavens angry for some reason. Don't make them even angrier by doing the wrong thing now.

[*Everybody goes out.*]

Act 5 Death in the Vault

Scene 1 A street in Mantua

[*Romeo comes in.*]

ROMEO: If I can believe in dreams, I'm going to get some good news soon. I dreamed that Juliet came. She found me dead. But she kissed me and I became alive again. Oh, how sweet are dreams of love! [*Balthasar arrives, wearing a coat and boots.*] News from Verona! How are you, Balthasar? Have you got any letters for me from the Friar? How is my lady? Is my father well? How is Juliet? Everything's all right if she's well.

BALTHASAR [*very sadly*]: Then she's well, and nothing is wrong. Her body is at rest in the Capulets' vault. And she's in heaven now. I came immediately to tell you.

ROMEO [*slowly*]: Juliet's dead? Is this really true? You know where I'm living. Get me a pen and paper. And find some horses. I'll leave here tonight. [*Balthasar leaves.*] Well, Juliet, I'll lie with you in death tonight. But how shall I kill myself? I remember a poor doctor who has a shop near here. I'm sure that he'll sell me some poison. Here's his house, as I remember. It's a holiday today and his shop is shut. [*calling*] Doctor!

[*The doctor arrives.*]

DOCTOR: Who's calling so loudly?

ROMEO [*showing him some pieces of gold*]: Here's some gold. I want to buy a very strong poison that can kill a man quickly.

DOCTOR: I have a poison like that. But I can't sell it to you. It's against the law of Mantua to sell strong poison.

ROMEO: You look very poor. You need this money.

DOCTOR: I really don't want to accept it. [*giving him the poison*] This poison is very strong. It will kill a man immediately.

ROMEO [*giving him the gold*]: There's your gold. More people in this world are murdered for gold than die by poison. Buy some food. Goodbye. [*The doctor leaves.*] I'll take this poison to Juliet's grave. I must use it there. [*He leaves.*]

Scene 2 *Friar Laurence's house*

[*Friar John comes in.*]

FRIAR JOHN: Friar Laurence! Brother!

[*Friar Laurence comes in.*]

FRIAR LAURENCE [*to himself*]: That's Friar John's voice. I sent him to Mantua with a letter for Romeo. [*to Friar John*] Welcome. What did Romeo say? Did he give you a letter for me?

FRIAR JOHN: I couldn't go to Mantua. I wanted another friar to travel with me, but he was visiting some sick people. Then the health officers of Verona came and closed the house. I couldn't leave.

FRIAR LAURENCE: So who took my letter to Romeo?

FRIAR JOHN: I couldn't find anybody to take it. Everybody was afraid of catching the terrible sickness. [*giving the letter to Friar Laurence*] Here's your letter back again.

FRIAR LAURENCE [*worried*]: This is very bad luck! There was some very important news for Romeo in that letter. Friar John, go and find me a strong crowbar. Bring it here immediately.

FRIAR JOHN: I'll find one for you, Brother. [*He goes out.*]

FRIAR LAURENCE: Now I'll have to go to the Capulets' vault alone. The lovely Juliet is going to wake up in the next three hours and Romeo won't be there. But I'll write to Romeo again. I'll keep Juliet here in my house until he arrives. Poor lady, shut in a vault with dead men!

Scene 3 The church garden with the Capulets' vault

[*Paris and his servant arrive, carrying a light and flowers.*]

PARIS: Give me your light, boy. Wait here in the church garden. No, put your light out. I don't want anybody to see me. Lie on the ground under those trees over there. Put your ear to the ground and listen. If you hear anybody, call quietly to me. Give me those flowers. Do as I tell you. Go!

SERVANT [*to himself*]: I'm afraid to stay here alone. But I'll try. [*He goes away.*]

PARIS [*going towards the vault*]: Sweet flower, I've come to put flowers on your grave. [*Paris's servant calls quietly.*] My boy's calling. Somebody's coming. But who? It's somebody with a light. I'll hide. [*He hides.*]

[*Romeo and Balthasar arrive, carrying a light and a crowbar.*]

ROMEO: Give me that crowbar. [*taking out a letter and giving it to Balthasar*] Take this letter in the morning to my father. Now give me the light. I'm breaking into the vault because I want to see Juliet's face again. And I want to take a ring from her dead finger. Go. If you watch me, I'll kill you.

BALTHASAR: I'll go, sir. I won't do anything to trouble you.

ROMEO: You're a good friend. [*giving him money*] Take this. Live, and be happy. Goodbye.

BALTHASAR [*to himself*]: I'm going to hide somewhere near. I think he's planning something terrible.

[*Balthasar hides. Romeo starts to break into the vault.*]

PARIS: This is that same proud Montague who murdered Tybalt, my love's cousin. Has he come to steal things from the vault? Stop, Montague! Come with me. You must die!

ROMEO: That's right, I have to die. That's why I came here. Listen, young man, don't make trouble for me. Don't make me angry – I don't want to hurt you. Just go away!

PARIS [*taking out his sword and attacking Romeo*]: No, I won't.

ROMEO: All right, then. [*taking out his sword and attacking Paris*] Take this, boy!

[*Paris and Romeo fight.*]

SERVANT: They're fighting! I'll go and call the guards.

[*The servant runs away. Paris is hurt and falls down.*]

PARIS: Oh, I'm dying! If you want to be kind, open the vault. Put my body next to Juliet's. [*He dies.*]

ROMEO: Yes, I will. Who is this young man? [*looking at him in surprise*] It's Mercutio's relative, the noble Paris! What did my servant tell me on the way here? Didn't he say that Paris wanted to marry Juliet? Or did I dream that? Or am I going crazy? [*taking Paris's hand*] Oh, give me your hand – you, a man as unlucky as I am. I'll put you in a fine grave. [*He opens the vault and sees Juliet's body.*] Here lies Juliet. She's so lovely. She fills this dark vault with light. [*He places Paris's body in the vault, then goes to Juliet.*] Oh, my love, my wife! There's still some colour in your lovely face. [*He sees Tybalt's body in the vault.*] Ah, Tybalt, are you lying there in your bloody clothes? I was the one who killed you. Now I'm going to kill myself. Forgive me, cousin! Ah, dear Juliet, why are you still so lovely? Eyes, look at Juliet for the last time! [*putting his arms round her*] Arms, hold her for the last time! [*kissing her*] And mouth, kiss her for the last time. Now, it's time for me to kill myself. [*He takes out the bottle of poison and drinks.*] Oh, doctor, you gave me a good strong poison. It's very quick. [*He kisses Juliet's hand.*] So, with a kiss, I die. [*He falls to the ground and dies.*]

[*Friar Laurence hurries into the church garden, carrying a light and a crowbar.*]

FRIAR: My old feet have fallen over a lot of graves tonight! [*He listens, then calls.*] Who's there?
BALTHASAR [*coming towards him*]: A man, sir, who knows you.
FRIAR [*surprised*]: Tell me, friend, what's that light there? I think it's burning in the Capulets' vault.
BALTHASAR: Yes, sir. My master is in there. He's somebody who you love.
FRIAR: Who's that?
BALTHASAR: Romeo.
FRIAR [*surprised*]: How long has he been there?

BALTHASAR: About half an hour.

FRIAR: Come into the vault with me.

BALTHASAR: I can't, sir. My master doesn't know that I'm here. He'll kill me if he finds me.

FRIAR: All right, then, stay here. I'll go alone. I feel very frightened. I'm afraid that something bad has happened.

BALTHASAR: As I was asleep under this tree, I had a dream. I dreamt that my master killed another man.

FRIAR [*going to the entrance of the vault*]: Romeo! [*He sees the blood and swords on the ground.*] Why is there blood on these stones? And what are these swords doing here? [*He goes into the vault and sees Romeo's body.*] Romeo! You're dead! [*He sees Paris's body.*] Who's this? Paris, too? Oh, what terrible thing has happened here? [*Juliet begins to move.*] And Juliet is waking up!

[*Juliet sits up.*]

JULIET: Oh, dear Friar! Where's Romeo? I'm in the right place. But where's my Romeo?

[*There is a noise outside.*]

FRIAR [*afraid*]: I hear a noise. Lady, come away from this place of death. Everything has gone wrong. Your husband lies dead, and Paris too. Don't stay to ask questions. The guards are coming. [*trying to pull Juliet with him*] Come away, dear Juliet. I'm afraid to stay here.

JULIET [*pushing him away*]: Go then! I'm not going to leave this place. [*The Friar goes out. Juliet sees Romeo's body on the ground. She falls on him and finds the bottle in his hand.*] What's this bottle in my true love's hand? [*She smells it.*] Poison! So that's how he died. Oh, my Romeo, haven't you left any for me? I'll kiss your mouth. Perhaps there's still some poison on it. Then I can taste it and join you in death. [*She kisses him.*] Your mouth is still warm!

FIRST GUARD [*from outside*]: You go first, boy. Which way?

JULIET: Do I hear a noise? Then I'll be quick. [*She sees Romeo's knife and picks it up.*] Oh, friendly knife! My body will be your final resting-place. [*She pushes the knife into her body and falls dead.*]

[*Paris's servant comes in with six guards.*]

SERVANT: This is the place. Here, where the light is burning.

FIRST GUARD [*to the other guards*]: The ground is covered with blood. Search the garden. Bring here anybody that you find. [*The second, third and fourth guards go out. The first guard sees the bodies.*] This is a very sad and strange thing! Here is Paris, lying dead. And Juliet! She died two days ago. But she lies here, warm and covered in blood. Go, tell the Prince. Run to the Capulets. Wake up the Montagues. [*The fifth and sixth guards go out. The second and third guards return with Balthasar.*]

SECOND GUARD: Here's Romeo's servant. We found him outside, in the church garden.

FIRST GUARD: Hold him safely until the Prince comes.

[*The fourth guard returns with Friar Laurence.*]

FOURTH GUARD: Here's a Friar who's very frightened. He was in the church garden, carrying a crowbar.

FIRST GUARD: Good! Hold the Friar too.

[*The Prince arrives with his servants.*]

PRINCE: What terrible accident has happened so early in the morning? Why have you woken me up?

[*Lord and Lady Capulet arrive with the fifth guard.*]

LORD CAPULET: What's all this noise about?

LADY CAPULET: People in the street are running towards our vault.

'Oh, friendly knife! My body will be your final resting-place.'

PRINCE: What has happened?

FIRST GUARD: Sir, Paris is lying here dead and Romeo is dead too. Juliet died two days ago, but her body is still warm.

PRINCE: Find out how these terrible murders happened.

FIRST GUARD: Here's a Friar, and Romeo's servant too. They have crowbars with them for breaking into the vault.

LORD CAPULET: Oh, wife, look at our daughter! The knife in her body is that Montague's knife.

LADY CAPULET: Oh, I want to die!

[*Lord Montague arrives with Abram and the sixth guard.*]

PRINCE: Come, Montague. You are here in time to see the dead body of your son.

LORD MONTAGUE: My wife died last night from sadness about Romeo's banishment. What other troubles must I suffer in my old age?

PRINCE [*pointing to Romeo's dead body*]: Look, and you will see.

LORD MONTAGUE: Oh, my son! You have died before me!

PRINCE: Do not say anything more. We must find out how these things happened. We will ask the Friar.

FRIAR: I didn't kill these young people, but I do know something about their deaths.

PRINCE: Then tell us immediately what you know.

FRIAR: I will tell you now. Romeo was Juliet's husband. I married them. When Tybalt was killed, Romeo was banished from Verona. Juliet was crying for Romeo, not for Tybalt. [*to Lord Capulet*] Then you wanted her to marry Paris. So she asked me to help her. I gave her a special medicine to drink. Everybody thought she was dead. Then I wrote to Romeo in Mantua and asked him to come. But Romeo didn't receive my letter, so I came to the vault alone. But when I arrived, I found the bodies of Romeo and Paris. Then Juliet woke up. I asked her to come with me but she refused. She stayed and killed herself. Her old nurse knows about this secret marriage too. If these young people have died because of me, then take my old life too.

PRINCE: We have always known you as a good friar. Where is Romeo's servant? What can he tell us?

BALTHASAR: I took the news of Juliet's death to my master in Mantua. He came immediately to this vault. [*taking out Romeo's letter*] He told me to give this letter to his father. Then he ordered me to leave and broke into the vault.

PRINCE: Give me the letter. [*Balthasar gives it to him.*] Where is Paris's servant? Why was your master here?

SERVANT: He came to put flowers on the lady Juliet's grave. Then a man came and broke into the vault. My master started fighting with him. So I ran away to call the guards.

PRINCE [*reading the letter*]: Romeo's letter describes his love for Juliet, and the news of her death. He bought a poison from a doctor in Mantua. Then he came here to kill himself. He wanted to lie in death with Juliet. [*looking round*] Where are these enemies? Capulet, Montague, see the terrible results of your hate. Your children are dead. And I could not stop your fights. So I, too, have lost some of my relatives. We are all punished now.

LORD CAPULET [*holding out his hand to Lord Montague*]: Give me your hand, brother Montague. Let's be friends. I cannot do any more for my daughter now.

LORD MONTAGUE [*taking Lord Capulet's hand*]: But I can. I will ask a painter to paint a picture of Juliet.

LORD CAPULET: I will do the same for Romeo. His picture will hang next to Juliet's in a building on the town square. Then everybody will know their story.

PRINCE [*to everybody*]: This morning has brought a grey kind of peace. The sun, from sadness, will not shine at all today. There was never a sadder story than this story of Romeo and Juliet.

[*Everybody leaves slowly. The guards carry out the bodies of Romeo, Juliet and Paris.*]

ACTIVITIES

Introduction and page viii

Before you read
1 What do you know about William Shakespeare?
   a Where in England was he born?
      Oxford   Bristol   Stratford
   b When was he born?
      1564   1664   1764
   c How many plays did he write?
      seven   twenty-seven   thirty-seven
2 Look at the Word List at the back of the book. Find the right words.
   a You can put this in someone's drink and kill them.
   b You can use this to open a strong metal door.
   c You do this to someone when you send them away.
   d An important person's body goes in here after they die.

While you read
3 Which is the right word?
   a Shakespeare's play about Romeo and Juliet ends *happily/sadly*.
   b Romeo and Juliet live in *Greece/Italy*.
   c Romeo's family and Juliet's family are great *friends/enemies*.
   d Shakespeare's plays were *never/always* successful.
   e He made *no money/a lot of money* from his plays.
   f The part of Juliet *is/was* always played by a boy.
   g Juliet's father is *Lord Montague/Lord Capulet*.
   h *Tybalt/Mercutio* is a relative of Juliet.

After you read
4 Do you know what happens in Shakespeare's story of Romeo and Juliet? Discuss the story with other students.

Act 1

Before you read
5 In the first scene, people from the Capulet family meet people from the Montague family in the street. What will happen, do you think?

While you read

6 Who wants to fight (✓)? Who doesn't want to fight (✗)?

Sampson	.....	Lord Capulet	.....
Abram	.....	Lord Montague	.....
Benvolio	.....	Lady Montague	.....
Tybalt	.....	Prince Escalus	.....
townspeople	.....		

7 Are these sentences right (✓) or wrong (✗)?

   a Romeo's parents know why Romeo shuts himself away. .....
   b Lord Montague wants Benvolio to talk to Romeo. .....
   c Romeo thinks that hate was the reason for the fight. .....
   d Romeo says he is in love with Juliet. .....

8 Find the right end to these sentences.

   a Paris wants to marry   a Montague.
   b Juliet is   brothers and sisters.
   c Juliet has no   a fine flower.
   d Peter doesn't know that Romeo is   Juliet.
   e Nurse and Lady Capulet think Paris is   thirteen.

9 Which of these happen at Lord Capulet's party (✓)?

   a Lord Capulet puts on a mask and dances. .....
   b Tybalt knows that Romeo is there. .....
   c Lord Capulet wants Tybalt to fight Romeo. .....
   d Romeo and Juliet fall in love. .....

After you read

10 Romeo falls in love with Juliet when he sees her for the first time. Does this happen in real life, do you think? Do you know of any examples? Discuss these questions.

11 Work with two other students. Have this conversation.

   Student A: You are very angry with Student B. Why? Tell him/her. Try to start a fight.
   Student B: You are angry with Student A. Tell him/her what you think. You are happy to fight.
   Student C: The other people are your friends and you don't want them to fight. Try to keep the peace.

Act 2

Before you read

12 At the beginning of Act 2, Romeo and Juliet meet secretly. Juliet is at her window. Romeo is in the garden below her window. What will they say, do you think?

While you read

13 Complete each sentence with one of these words.

safe   sun   cold   messenger   soon   different

   a Mercutio and Benvolio go home because the night is ....

   b Romeo says that Juliet is like the ....

   c Juliet is unhappy that Romeo doesn't have a .... name.

   d Romeo is not .... in Juliet's garden.

   e Juliet thinks this meeting in her garden has come too ....

   f Juliet will send a .... to Romeo at nine o'clock in the morning.

14 What does Friar Laurence do (✓)?

   gets up late   .....   marries people   .....
   finds plants   .....   helps people with their problems   .....

15 How are these people described? Find the correct words on the right.

   a Tybalt   a fine man
   b Nurse   a rude boy
   c Mercutio   a strange-looking person
   d Romeo   the sweetest lady
   e Juliet   an excellent swordsman
   f Paris   a true gentleman

16 Friar Laurence marries Romeo and Juliet at the end of Act 2. How long ago did the two young people meet for the first time (✓)?

   less than a day .....   a day .....   more than a day .....

After you read

17 Answer these questions.
   a Why is Juliet unhappy about Romeo's name?
   b Why does Friar Laurence agree to help Romeo and Juliet?
   c Why does Mercutio make fun of the Nurse?
   d Why does Juliet get so cross with the Nurse when she returns from her meeting with Romeo?

18 Read Scene 4 again. Work with another student. Have this conversation.
   Student A: Like the Nurse, you have some news but you want to talk about other things first.
   Student B: Like Juliet, you want to hear the news. You are not interested in any other subjects.

Act 3 Scenes 1–2

Before you read

19 Romeo and Juliet are married and in love. Should they tell their families, do you think? Will they? Discuss these questions.

20 Act 3 is called 'Murder and Banishment'. Who is going to die? Who is going to leave the city? What do you think? Tell the class.

While you read

21 There are three crimes and three punishments in Scene 1. What are they? Who are the criminals and who punishes them? Complete this table.

Who?	Crime	Punishment	Who by?
	starts a fight with Tybalt		Tybalt
Tybalt		killed	
		banished	

57

22 How does Juliet feel at these times? Choose from these words:
excited   worried   she wants to die   happy   sad
   a She thinks Romeo is coming.   ....
   b She sees Nurse's unhappy face.   ....
   c She thinks Romeo is dead.   ....
   d She learns that Romeo is alive.   ....
   e She learns that Romeo is banished.   ....

After you read

23 What one thing happens that changes everything for Romeo and Juliet?

24 Benvolio describes what happened between Mercutio, Tybalt and Romeo to the Prince. What lie does he tell?

25 Discuss how the Prince and the people of Verona can stop the fighting between the Capulets and the Montagues. Write down two suggestions. Do other students have different suggestions?

Act 3 Scenes 3–5

Before you read

26 Discuss these questions. What do you think?
   a Will Romeo and Juliet ever meet again?
   b Romeo has a lot of problems now. Will he be strong or weak?

While you read

27 Friar Laurence tells Romeo his plan. What does he say first? Number these sentences, 1–5.
   a Go with her to Mantua.   .....
   b Come back to Verona.   .....
   c Go to Juliet.   .....
   d I'll tell everyone about your marriage.   .....
   e The Price will forgive you.   .....

28 Are these sentences right (✓) or wrong (✗)?
   a Juliet's parents think she is sad about Tybalt. .....
   b Paris and Juliet's wedding will be on Wednesday. .....
   c There will be a big party with lots of guests. .....
   d Romeo and Juliet spend the night together. .....
   e Lady Capulet brings news that makes Juliet happy. .....
   f If Juliet refuses to marry Paris, her father will throw her out of his house. .....

After you read

29 Friar Laurence thinks of three reasons for Romeo to be happy. What are they?

30 Juliet is the Capulets' only child. They say they will throw her out if she does not marry Paris. What happens when *you* don't agree with *your* parents? Talk to another student.

Act 4

Before you read

31 Will Juliet marry Paris on Thursday, do you think? Why (not)?

While you read

32 Complete each sentence with one word.
   a Juliet will kill herself with a .... if Friar Laurence doesn't help her.
   b After Juliet drinks the .... , she will sleep for .... hours.
   c Paris will think she is ....
   d Her family will take her body to the Capulets' ....
   e Friar Laurence will send a friar to Mantua with a .... for Romeo.

33 Which of these does Lord Capulet ask people to do for the wedding (✓)?

invite the guests	.....	bring flowers into the house	.....
buy wine	.....	bring dry wood for the fire	.....
find twenty excellent cooks	.....	make a large cake	.....

34 Find the right end to these sentences.
   a Nurse   says Juliet is like the sweetest flower.
   b Lord Capulet   thinks he has lost his love and his life.
   c Lady Capulet   knows Juliet is still alive.
   d Friar Laurence   thinks Death has taken her only child.
   e Paris   finds Juliet's body on the bed.

After you read

35 Work with another student. Imagine that Romeo meets Paris at Friar Laurence's. Have this conversation.
   Student A: You are Paris. Tell Romeo that you are going to marry Juliet on Thursday.
   Student B: You are Romeo. Ask Paris questions. Tell him what you think.

Act 5

Before you read

36 Talk to another student. Do you think Friar Laurence's plan will work? Why (not)? Can you think of a better plan?

37 Which of these people do you think will still be alive at the end of the play?

Benvolio   Romeo   Lord Capulet   Lady Montague   Friar Laurence   Juliet   the Prince

While you read

38 What happens first? Number these sentences, 1–7.
   a Balthasar tells Romeo that Juliet is dead.   .....
   b Friar Laurence learns that his letter didn't reach Romeo. .....
   c Juliet finds Romeo's body and the empty poison bottle.   .....
   d Juliet kills herself with the knife.   .....
   e Romeo and Paris fight in the church garden.   .....
   f Romeo buys some strong poison.   .....
   g Romeo finds Juliet's body and drinks the poison.   .....
39 How many newly-dead bodies are in the vault?   .....
   Who are they? ....
   ....

After you read

40 What do the Montagues and Capulets decide to do to remember the sad story of Romeo and Juliet?

Writing

41 You are a reporter for the *Verona Times*. You are at Lord Capulet's party in Act 1. Write a report about the party: Who was there? What did they wear? What did the room look like? What happened?

42 You saw Mercutio's and Tybalt's murders at the end of Act 3 Scene 1. Write a report about the scene for the police.

43 At the end of Act 4 Scene 1, Friar Laurence sends a letter to Romeo in Mantua. He tells him his plan to save Juliet. Write the Friar's letter.

44 At the end of the play, Balthasar has a letter that Romeo wrote to his father. The Prince reads it. Write Romeo's letter.

45 The Nurse goes into the kitchen at the Capulet house after the terrible scenes in the vault. She tells the cook the story. Write their conversation.

46 Write about Romeo or Juliet. What kind of person was he/she?

47 *Romeo and Juliet* ends very sadly. Change the ending of the story to make it happier.

48 Describe how life in Verona changes for the townspeople after the deaths of Romeo and Juliet.

49 You are a newspaper reporter. You went to see the play last night at a theatre in your home town. Write about it for your readers.

50 There are many unhappy love stories from around the world. Think of one you know or find out about one. Write the story.

Answers for the Activities in this book are available from the Pearson English Readers website. A free Activity Worksheet is also available from the website. Activity worksheets are part of the Pearson English Readers Teacher Support Programme, which also includes Progress tests and Graded Reader Guidelines. For more information, please visit:
www.pearsonenglishreaders.com

WORD LIST

act (n) one of the main parts of a play
banish (v) to punish someone by sending them away
character (n) a person in a play
crowbar (n) a strong metal bar used for opening things
curse (n) words to bring someone bad luck
friar (n) a religious man who teaches people about the Christian religion
gentleman (n) a man from a good family or a man who is good and polite
grave (n) a place under the ground where a body is put after death
heaven (n) the place where good people go after death
lord (n) a man with a high position because of the family that he comes from
mask (n) something that covers all or part of your face
master (n) the employer of a person who works in his house
noble (adj) good and kind, or from an important family
peace (n) a time without fighting, or a state of calm
poison (n/v) something that can kill people or animals. For example, there are poisons in some plants and in the bites of some animals.
rope (n) something strong and thick that you use for tying things
scene (n) a short part of a play
servant (n) someone who works in another person's house
sword (n) a long, sharp piece of metal like a big knife, used for fighting
vault (n) a room where the bodies of people from the same family are put after their deaths

Better learning
comes from fun.

Pearson English **Readers**

There are plenty of Pearson English Readers to choose from - world classics, film and television adaptations, short stories, thrillers, modern-day crime and adventure, biographies, American classics, non-fiction, plays ... and more to come.

For a complete list of all Pearson English Readers titles, please contact your local Pearson Education office or visit the website.

pearsonenglishreaders.com

LONGMAN
Dictionaries

Express yourself with confidence

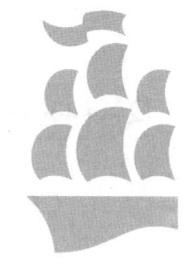

Longman has led the way in ELT dictionaries since 1935. We constantly talk to students and teachers around the world to find out what they need from a learners' dictionary.

Why choose a Longman dictionary?

EASY TO UNDERSTAND

Longman invented the Defining Vocabulary - 2000 of the most common words which are used to write the definitions in our dictionaries. So Longman definitions are always clear and easy to understand.

REAL, NATURAL ENGLISH

All Longman dictionaries contain natural examples taken from real-life that help explain the meaning of a word and show you how to use it in context.

AVOID COMMON MISTAKES

Longman dictionaries are written specially for learners, and we make sure that you get all the help you need to avoid common mistakes. We analyse typical learners' mistakes and include notes on how to avoid them.

DIGITAL INNOVATION

Longman dictionaries are also available online at:
www.longmandictionaries.com or **www.longmandictionariesusa.com**

These are premier dictionary websites that allow you to access the best of Longman Learners' dictionaries, whatever you do, wherever you are. They offer a wealth of additional resources for teachers and students in the Teacher's Corner and the Study Centre.